Guardians of the Waters

Preserving the Legacy of Caiman Crocodiles

MARY F. CARION

Table of Contents

Chapter One..4

Introduction 4

Brief history of the relationship between humans and caiman crocodiles....................8

Chapter Two 13

The Biology and Ecology of Caiman Crocodiles 13

ecological functions that caiman crocodiles perform in their environments and the significance of preserving their populations 17

Chapter Three 25

Conservation Efforts for Caiman Crocodiles 25

challenges and successes of these efforts, and the role of captive breeding programs in conservation. 30

Chapter Four...36

Threats to Caiman Crocodiles 36

Chapter Five...46

The Future of Caiman Crocodiles...............46

Chapter Six...56

Caiman Crocodiles and Human Culture 56

How changing attitudes towards caiman crocodiles affects their conservation status 61

Chapter Seven..67

Ethical Considerations in Caiman Crocodile Conservation...67

Conclusion...77

Chapter One
Introduction

An iconic species of crocodilians that is native to the Caribbean and areas of South and Central America are caiman crocodiles. From ancient indigenous societies who venerated them as sacred animals to contemporary communities who depend on them for food and revenue, these remarkable creatures have long interacted with people.

Although they are important to culture, caiman crocodiles are threatened with extinction on a large scale. The International Union for Conservation of Nature (IUCN) presently lists them as a vulnerable species, with population decreases and habitat degradation as the main causes.

In light of these dangers and difficulties, the goal of this book is to examine the future of caiman crocodiles. We'll look at the situation of caiman crocodiles and possible solutions to ensure their existence through a combination of scientific investigation, conservation activities, and cultural concerns.

The biology, ecology, natural habitats, and behavior of caiman crocodiles will all be covered in this book, along with the conservation measures being made to preserve their populations. We'll also look at the numerous dangers that caiman crocodiles face, like habitat loss, poaching, and climate change, and talk about how these dangers can affect their populations.

Finally, we will look at the ethical issues surrounding the conservation of caiman crocodiles, such as concerns with animal welfare, environmental protection, and public safety. We will take into account various viewpoints on these problems and investigate alternative solutions for juggling conflicting ethical worries.

In general, this book is written for everyone with an interest in what becomes of caiman crocodiles, including researchers, conservationists, and members of the general public as well as policymakers. We can take steps to ensure that caiman crocodiles survive for many generations by looking at the existing situation and potential solutions for safeguarding these amazing animals.

Brief history of the relationship between humans and caiman crocodiles

Caiman crocodiles were venerated and even worshiped as sacred animals in numerous civilizations during the early stages of human civilisation. The caiman crocodile, for instance, was worshipped as a deity of fertility and water by the ancient Mayans, and the Aztecs featured them in their artwork and thought they possessed magical abilities.

Caiman crocodiles were heavily killed later, during the colonial era, for their hides, which were highly sought-after for leather items. Due to massive population losses caused by this, caiman crocodiles were widely regarded as endangered by the middle of the 20th century.

But since then, major attempts have been made to safeguard caiman crocodiles and their natural habitats. Programs for conservation, habitat restoration, and the creation of protected areas have all been a part of these initiatives. As a result, certain places have seen a recovery in caiman crocodile numbers.

The topics that will be covered in this book include:

- The biology and ecology of caiman crocodiles

- The conservation efforts being made to protect caiman crocodiles and their habitats

- The various threats facing caiman crocodiles, including habitat loss, poaching, and climate change

- The future of caiman crocodiles in light of these threats and challenges

- The role of caiman crocodiles in human culture, from traditional beliefs and practices to contemporary art and media

- The ethical considerations involved in caiman crocodile conservation

In order to provide a thorough overview of the existing situation and prospective solutions for safeguarding caiman crocodiles, we will cover these topics in depth throughout the book.

Chapter Two

The Biology and Ecology of Caiman Crocodiles

A unique and fascinating species of crocodilian is the caiman crocodile. With adult males growing to an average length of around 2.5 meters and females to an average length of about 1.8 meters, they are typically smaller than other crocodilian species. They have a peculiar snout with a flattened shape that is well-suited for grabbing prey, a V-shaped ridge on top of their skull, and other distinguishing features.

Caiman crocodiles have a number of physiological modifications that enable them to live in their ecological settings. For their survival in brackish or salty conditions, they have a particular salt gland that enables them to expel extra salt from their bodies. Additionally, they have an unusual respiration mechanism that enables them to remain underwater for extended periods of time.

There are many different habitats where caiman crocodiles can be found, such as freshwater rivers, mangrove swamps, and even coastal areas. Throughout their lifespan, they are known to switch between several habitat types. Generally speaking, caiman crocodiles favor areas with an abundance of prey and appropriate breeding locations.

Caiman crocodiles are recognized for their distinctive vocalizations, which they utilize to communicate with other individuals. Additionally, they exhibit intricate social behavior, with females frequently protecting their nests and young from predators. Male caiman crocodiles ferociously defend their territories from other males, and they are also renowned for their aggressive territorial nature.

In general, conserving caiman crocodiles requires an understanding of their biology and environment. We can create efficient protection plans for them and their habitats by comprehending their physiological and behavioral adaptations as well as their natural habitats and habits.

ecological functions that caiman crocodiles perform in their environments and the significance of preserving their populations

Caiman crocodiles play important ecological roles in their ecosystems. As top predators, they help to control the populations of prey species, which can have cascading effects on the entire ecosystem. For example, in freshwater rivers and wetlands, caiman crocodiles help to regulate fish populations, which can in turn affect the abundance of plant species and other animals in the ecosystem.

Caiman crocodiles are also important nutrient recyclers, as they consume a variety of prey species and their waste products can provide nutrients to other organisms in the ecosystem. In addition, their burrows and nests can provide shelter for other animals, such as turtles and birds.

Protecting caiman crocodile populations is important not only for the species itself but also for the overall health and stability of the ecosystems in which they live. By conserving caiman crocodiles and their habitats, we can help to maintain the balance of ecosystems and ensure the survival of other species that depend on them.

In addition, caiman crocodiles have cultural and economic significance for many local communities. They are a source of food, medicine, and other materials, and have traditional spiritual and cultural significance in many regions. Protecting caiman crocodiles can therefore also help to support local communities and promote sustainable development.

Caiman crocodiles have roles other than being top predators and are significant ecological contributors to the habitats they live in. Caiman crocodiles are keystone species in many ecosystems, which means that, compared to their abundance, their presence and behaviors have a disproportionately large impact on the ecosystem's structure and function. As apex predators, they contribute to maintaining the overall health and diversity of the ecosystem by keeping prey species' populations under control and preventing overgrazing and overbrowsing.

The management of fish populations in freshwater settings is one of the most significant functions of caiman crocodiles. Caiman crocodiles eat a variety of fish species and have a strong affinity for fish. Because of this predation, fish populations are kept in check and overconsumption of some species, which could cause ecological imbalances, is prevented. This is crucial in freshwater systems like wetlands, which frequently support a diverse range of fish species.

Another important player in the cycling of nutrients is the caiman crocodile. As they consume a wide range of prey species, their waste materials give plants and algae, among other organisms in the ecosystem, vital nutrients. The ecosystem's productivity is supported by this nutrient recycling, which also fosters the expansion of other species.

The construction of habitat is another crucial function of caiman crocodiles. Burrows and nests dug by caiman crocodiles serve as vital habitats and havens for other species, including turtles and birds. Additionally, these structures aid in the creation of crucial microhabitats for a range of ecosystem-dependent creatures.

To preserve the biological integrity of their habitats and the general health of the ecosystems they live in, it is crucial to protect caiman crocodile populations. Threats to caiman crocodile populations and their habitats include overfishing, habitat loss, and pollution. We can contribute to ensuring the viability of the habitats in which they exist and preserving the diversity of species that rely on them by preserving these populations.

Caiman crocodiles provide important ecological responsibilities as well as cultural and monetary ones. They have historical spiritual and cultural value and are a source of food, medicine, and other resources in many places. Thus, protecting caiman crocodiles can also aid in fostering sustainable development and aiding local populations.

Chapter Three

Conservation Efforts for Caiman Crocodiles

There have been numerous national and international initiatives to conserve caiman crocodiles, as well as local community-based conservation programs. Protecting caiman crocodiles and their habitats from challenges including habitat loss, overfishing, and pollution is the main goal of these conservation activities.

Protecting habitat is one of the most important conservation methods for caiman crocodiles. Numerous sites, including wetlands and rivers, that are crucial for caiman crocodile populations have been classified as protected zones, where activities like fishing, hunting, and development are prohibited. These protected areas help to preserve the integrity of the ecosystems in which caiman crocodiles thrive in addition to provide a safe sanctuary for them.

Programs for captive breeding and reintroduction of caiman crocodiles have also been put in place to support population growth in addition to habitat protection. These initiatives entail raising people in captivity, reproducing them, and then releasing them into the wild. This increases both the total number of individuals in the population and the genetic diversity of wild populations.

Community-based conservation initiatives are a crucial component of the caiman crocodile's conservation. These initiatives collaborate with neighborhood communities to support conservation efforts and advocate the sustainable use of natural resources. These projects frequently offer communities incentives to safeguard caiman crocodiles and their habitats, such as through fostering ecotourism or supporting cultural practices that depend on the animal.

The protection of caiman crocodiles has also received international attention. For instance, in order to prevent overexploitation and guarantee the sustainability of commerce, the Convention on International commerce in Endangered Species of Wild Fauna and Flora (CITES) controls the international trade of caiman crocodiles and their products, such as skins and flesh.

Overall, caiman crocodile conservation efforts have been successful in many locations, and some localities have seen an increase in population as a result. Nevertheless, there is still more work to be done because threats to the species, like habitat loss and overhunting, continue to present serious obstacles. The long-term survival of caiman crocodiles and the ecosystems they inhabit depends on continued conservation initiatives, including as habitat protection, captive breeding and reintroduction projects, community-based conservation, and international trade rules.

challenges and successes of these efforts, and the role of captive breeding programs in conservation.

While conservation efforts for caiman crocodiles have made significant progress in recent years, there are still a number of challenges that remain. Some of the major challenges to caiman crocodile conservation include:

1. Habitat loss and degradation: The loss and degradation of wetland and river habitats

remain a major threat to caiman crocodile populations, particularly in areas where human populations are rapidly expanding.

2. Overhunting: Caiman crocodiles are still hunted for their meat and skins in many parts of their range, despite protections afforded to them by law. Overhunting can deplete populations and create imbalances in the ecosystem.

3. Climate change: As temperatures rise and weather patterns shift, caiman crocodile populations could be significantly impacted. Changes in temperature and rainfall patterns can alter their habitat and food sources.

Despite these challenges, there have been a number of successes in caiman crocodile conservation efforts. For example:

1. Populations of some caiman crocodile species have

increased in certain areas due to habitat protection and the implementation of conservation measures.

2. CITES regulations have helped to regulate the international trade in caiman crocodiles and their products, which has helped to reduce overhunting and overexploitation of populations.

3. Community-based conservation programs have been successful in some regions in promoting

sustainable use of natural resources and increasing awareness about the importance of conserving caiman crocodiles and their habitats.

Captive breeding programs have also played an important role in caiman crocodile conservation. These programs involve breeding individuals in captivity and then releasing them into the wild to bolster wild populations. Captive breeding programs can help to increase genetic diversity in wild populations, and can also be used as a tool to reintroduce species to areas where they have been extirpated. However, captive breeding programs are not a substitute for habitat protection and other conservation measures, as they can be expensive and resource-intensive. Additionally, it is important to ensure that captive-bred individuals are genetically diverse and adapted to survive in the wild before they are released.

Chapter Four

Threats to Caiman Crocodiles

Caiman crocodiles face a variety of threats to their survival, including:

1. Habitat loss and degradation: Wetlands and riverine habitats where caiman crocodiles live are often threatened by human activities such as agriculture, mining, and urbanization. As these habitats are destroyed or altered, the crocodiles lose important nesting sites and

hunting grounds, which can lead to declines in population.

2. Poaching: Caiman crocodiles are hunted for their meat and skin, which are highly valued in many parts of the world. Poaching can have a severe impact on caiman crocodile populations, particularly in areas where enforcement of wildlife laws is weak.

3. Climate change: Climate change is likely to have a significant impact on caiman crocodile populations in the

future. Rising temperatures and changes in rainfall patterns could affect the availability of prey species, as well as the quality and quantity of nesting sites.

4. Water pollution: Pollution of waterways where caiman crocodiles live can have a range of negative impacts on their health and reproduction. Pesticides and other chemicals can accumulate in their tissues, and oil spills can contaminate their habitat.

5. Human-crocodile conflict: As human populations expand and encroach on crocodile habitat, conflicts between humans and crocodiles can arise. This can lead to the killing of crocodiles, which can have a negative impact on population size and structure.

6. Invasive species: Invasive species such as the common myna (a bird species) can prey on the eggs and young of caiman crocodiles, reducing their reproductive success.

In general, the threats that caiman crocodiles confront are intricate and linked, therefore resolving them will necessitate a multidimensional strategy. To lessen human-crocodile conflict, conservation activities must concentrate on protecting habitat, regulating trade and hunting, and providing education and outreach. In order to combat climate change, efforts must be made to cut greenhouse gas emissions and boost adaptation measures. Coordination of conservation activities across national and international borders is crucial, as is participation of local populations, government agencies, and conservation groups.

Depending on the region and species, the dangers impacting caiman crocodile populations have had various effects. However, because of these dangers, populations have decreased in many locations. For instance, the IUCN Red List has designated the black caiman (Melanosuchus niger) as Vulnerable because to habitat loss, poaching, and over-exploitation. Comparably, the Spectacled caiman (Caiman crocodilus) has been rated as Least Concern, however habitat degradation and hunting have resulted to population decreases in some places.

Conservation efforts must be directed at tackling the underlying causes of these problems in order to lessen their impact on caiman crocodile populations. The protection of habitat is a crucial part of conservation efforts, and it's crucial to create protected areas and preserve the wetlands and riverine ecosystems that are essential to the survival of caiman crocodiles. Additionally, laws must be passed to control commerce and hunting, and enforcement must be stepped up to stop poaching.

Attempts to lessen confrontation between humans and crocodiles are also crucial. This can involve supporting alternative occupations that do not require hunting or habitat degradation as well as teaching local populations about the value of caiman crocodiles. In addition to encouraging conservation, the adoption of sustainable tourism can help local people economically.

Finally, efforts to lower greenhouse gas emissions and support adaptation measures are necessary to combat climate change. This can involve activities like planting new trees to store carbon, encouraging the use of renewable energy sources, and creating crop kinds resistant to drought.

Governments, conservation groups, and local communities will need to work together to mitigate the threats to caiman crocodile populations. We can guarantee the continuation of these significant and distinctive species by cooperating to address the underlying causes of these dangers.

Chapter Five

The Future of Caiman Crocodiles

The success of conservation initiatives will determine the future of caiman crocodiles. As a result of habitat loss, poaching, and climate change, some populations have begun to show indications of recovery, while others are still in decline. There are, however, causes for optimism.

The growing understanding of the significance of caiman crocodiles in their ecosystems is one encouraging development. As top predators, caiman crocodiles are crucial for regulating prey populations and preserving the ecological balance. Therefore, protecting them is crucial for both their own existence and the health and wellbeing of the ecosystems in which they dwell.

The rising understanding of the dangers caiman crocodiles face and the necessity of taking action to protect them is another cause for optimism. Caiman crocodiles and their habitats are being safeguarded by governments, conservation groups, and local communities through initiatives including protected areas, hunting restrictions, and community-based conservation programs.

However, difficulties persist. To lessen their effects on caiman crocodile populations, climate change and habitat degradation must be addressed urgently. In order to discourage illicit hunting and trading, enforcement activities must be stepped up as poaching is still a constant concern.

The protection of these vital species and their habitats by individuals, groups, and governments will ultimately determine the fate of caiman crocodiles. We can guarantee that caiman crocodiles have a sustainable, safe, and prosperous future if we keep cooperating.

Climate change is one of the most significant threats to caiman crocodile populations, with potential impacts on their habitats, behavior, and survival. Some of the potential effects of climate change on caiman crocodiles include:

1. Habitat loss: Rising sea levels and changes in precipitation patterns can lead to the loss of wetland and riverine habitats critical for caiman crocodile survival.

2. Changes in temperature: Increasing temperatures can alter the nesting behavior and sex ratios of caiman crocodiles, affecting population dynamics.

3. Increased frequency of extreme weather events: Floods and droughts can affect the availability of prey and the suitability of nesting sites.

To mitigate the impacts of climate change on caiman crocodile populations, several potential solutions can be explored:

1. Habitat protection and restoration: Protecting and

restoring wetland and riverine habitats can help ensure that caiman crocodiles have access to suitable nesting sites, foraging areas, and other resources.

2. Captive breeding and reintroduction programs: Captive breeding programs can help maintain genetic diversity and provide a source of individuals for reintroduction into areas where populations have declined due to climate change or other threats.

3.   Conservation   planning:
Incorporating   climate   change
projections   into   conservation
planning can help identify areas that
may be most vulnerable to climate
change and prioritize conservation
efforts accordingly.

4. Sustainable management   of
natural   resources: Promoting
sustainable management of natural
resources, such as fisheries and
timber, can help reduce pressure on
caiman   crocodile   habitats   and
promote their long-term survival.

5. Education and outreach: Education and outreach efforts can help raise awareness about the impacts of climate change on caiman crocodiles and promote actions to reduce greenhouse gas emissions and adapt to changing environmental conditions.

Addressing the impacts of climate change on caiman crocodile populations will require a multi-faceted approach that integrates conservation, research, and policy efforts. By working together to address the root causes of climate change and promote sustainable management practices, we can help ensure a future for caiman crocodiles and the ecosystems they inhabit.

Chapter Six

Caiman Crocodiles and Human Culture

For thousands of years, caiman crocodiles have been a key part of human civilization. Caiman crocodiles are revered as sacred creatures in numerous indigenous South and Central American cultures, and a number of rituals and activities are connected to them. For instance, caiman crocodiles are revered as strong spirits and regarded as the water's keepers in several civilizations. They are linked to creation myths or revered for their curative qualities in various cultures.

Caiman crocodiles have been used in traditional activities including hunting and healing in addition to their spiritual significance. For their nutritional and therapeutic benefits, caiman crocodile meat and skin are highly prized in various cultures. Products made from caiman crocodiles have been used in traditional medicine in a number of nations, including Brazil, Colombia, and Peru.

Crocodiles from the Caiman Islands have served as a significant source of inspiration for modern art and media. For instance, caiman crocodile leather is highly valued for both its strength and beauty, and it is used to create upscale products like handbags, shoes, and belts. Additionally, caiman crocodiles have been included in a number of movies, books, and documentaries, such as nature films that emphasize their significance to the environment and the necessity of conservation efforts.

The traditional importance of caiman crocodiles has, however, also encouraged unsustainably aggressive activities like overhunting and poaching. Due to the high demand for their skin and meat, caiman crocodile populations in some areas have been wiped out. Therefore, it is crucial to continue conservation efforts to guarantee the survival of caiman crocodiles and their cultural relevance.

In conclusion, caiman crocodiles have been significant to human culture for a very long time. Even though they were considered as sacred creatures in many indigenous cultures, they were also used in customs and served as an inspiration for modern art and media. The sustainability of caiman crocodile populations, however, as well as its cultural significance, are under danger because to unsustainable activities like overhunting and poaching. To ensure that caiman crocodiles remain a part of human culture for many years to come, it is crucial to support sustainable practices and conservation activities.

How changing attitudes towards caiman crocodiles affects their conservation status

The conservation status of caiman crocodiles can be significantly impacted by shifting attitudes about them. In the past, caiman crocodiles were frequently seen as nuisances and risks to people's safety and way of life, which resulted in extensive hunting and habitat devastation. The necessity for caiman crocodile protection and its significance to the ecology, however, have come to the forefront in recent years.

Through education and outreach initiatives, one way to raise public interest in and involvement in caiman crocodile protection is. These initiatives might involve speaking at public events, visiting schools, and running social media campaigns to educate people about the dangers that caiman crocodiles face and how important they are to the environment. By raising public awareness, it might be able to persuade more people to support conservation efforts, both individually (by decreasing plastic waste, for example) and collectively (by funding habitat protection and restoration programs, for example).

Ecotourism is another means of boosting interest in caiman crocodile conservation among the general population. Ecotourism can give local governments financial motivation to assist conservation initiatives and safeguard caiman crocodile habitats. Ecotourism can help promote awareness of the value of conservation efforts and the need to safeguard these species and their habitats by giving tourists the chance to see caiman crocodiles in their natural setting.

And finally, it's critical to involve neighborhood groups in caiman crocodile conservation initiatives.

For example, through tourist or hunting, many local communities rely on caiman crocodile populations for their livelihoods. It might be possible to promote conservation while simultaneously helping local economies and communities by incorporating local communities in conservation initiatives and offering financial incentives for sustainable behaviors.

In conclusion, the conservation status of caiman crocodiles may significantly change if views toward them change. Promoting caiman crocodile conservation and safeguarding these significant species and their ecosystems could be accomplished by raising public awareness and encouraging participation through outreach, education, and ecotourism as well as through interacting with local communities.

Chapter Seven

Ethical Considerations in Caiman Crocodile Conservation

The conservation of caiman crocodiles raises several moral questions, such as those of animal care, environmental protection, and public safety.

The welfare of individual animals used in conservation initiatives is a significant ethical factor. While caiman crocodile populations are the focus of conservation efforts, it's crucial to make sure that individual animals are respected and cared for. This entails reducing the strain and trauma brought on by capture and transportation, offering the right kind of food and shelter, and making sure that animals are released into acceptable habitats.

The possible effects of conservation efforts on other species and the larger environment are another ethical factor. Examples of unexpected effects of captive breeding operations include the loss of genetic diversity or the possibility of spreading illness to wild populations. To ensure that conservation efforts are founded on good scientific principles, it is crucial to thoroughly assess the potential effects of conservation efforts on other species and ecosystems.

In the ethical context of caiman crocodile conservation, public safety is thus crucial. Even though caiman crocodiles are an essential component of many ecosystems, they may also be dangerous to people, especially in locations where human settlements and their habitats mix. The desire to safeguard caiman crocodiles must be balanced with the need to maintain public safety, for instance by putting warning signs up, putting up fence, and moving problem animals.

There may be conflicting viewpoints and issues at stake when it comes to ethical issues in caiman crocodile conservation. Some conservationists, for instance, could put the welfare of individual animals above the safety of the general public, whilst others might put the welfare of human populations above the welfare of individual animals. There are several possible methods that might be taken into account to reconcile these conflicting interests.

Prioritizing the use of non-lethal techniques for controlling caiman crocodile populations is one possible option. This can be done through techniques like moving problematic animals, putting up fences and obstacles to keep people and crocodiles apart, and running public awareness programs to raise understanding of the dangers and proper conduct around caiman crocodiles. By using these techniques, it might be able to lessen the threat to human populations while reducing damage to certain animals.

Prioritizing the preservation of caiman crocodile populations in their natural environments is another option. Without the need for major management interventions, it may be able to sustain healthy populations of caiman crocodiles by safeguarding natural ecosystems and reducing human encroachment. Additionally, through fostering ecosystem health and resilience, this can benefit other species and the environment as a whole.

Engaging local stakeholders and communities can also be a good method to balance conflicting ethical concerns. Finding solutions that balance the requirements of various stakeholders may be achieved by including communities in conservation initiatives and paying attention to their concerns. For instance, it may be possible to help local economies while promoting conservation by collaborating with local communities to create sustainable tourist initiatives that prioritize the health of caiman crocodiles and enhance public safety.

In conclusion, the conservation of caiman crocodiles raises several moral questions about animal welfare, environmental protection, and community security. The possible effects of conservation efforts should be thoroughly assessed, and it is crucial to make sure that these efforts are supported by solid scientific concepts, as well as by considerations for the wellbeing of specific animals and the security of human populations. It might be conceivable to advance efficient caiman crocodile conservation while also respecting the requirements and interests of other species and human groups by balancing these ethical factors.

Balancing competing ethical issues in the conservation of the caiman crocodile necessitates careful evaluation of many viewpoints and a willingness to interact with stakeholders in order to create solutions that satisfy various stakeholder groups. It might be able to advance effective conservation while also respecting the requirements and interests of other species and human societies by giving non-lethal techniques for managing caiman crocodile numbers, safeguarding natural ecosystems, and interacting with local communities.

Conclusion

In conclusion, this book has explored the biology, ecology, conservation, and cultural significance of caiman crocodiles. Through this exploration, we have seen that caiman crocodiles play an important ecological role in their natural habitats, but are facing significant threats from habitat loss, poaching, and climate change.

Despite these challenges, we have also seen that there are many conservation efforts underway to protect caiman crocodiles and their habitats. These efforts have had some successes, but there is still much work to be done to ensure the long-term survival of these vulnerable species.

As individuals and organizations, we can all play a role in caiman crocodile conservation. This can include supporting conservation organizations, advocating for stronger conservation policies, and making responsible choices in our daily lives that minimize our impact on the environment. We can also work to increase public awareness and engagement with caiman crocodile conservation, through education, outreach, and advocacy efforts.

Ultimately, the future of caiman crocodiles depends on our collective actions. By coming together to protect these remarkable creatures and their habitats, we can ensure that they continue to thrive for generations to come. Let us all commit to this important cause and work towards a future where caiman crocodiles and their ecosystems are protected and celebrated.